For Janet
~G.R.
For my grandchild
~M.P.

First American edition published 2000 by
CROCODILE BOOKS, USA
An imprint of Interlink Publishing Group, Inc.
99 Seventh Avenue, Brooklyn, New York 11215 and
46 Crosby Street, Northampton, Massachusetts 01060
www.interlinkbooks.com

Text © 2000 Maggie Pearson
Illustrations © 2000 Gavin Rowe

Printed in Singapore
All rights reserved • ISBN 1-56656-377-1

The HEADLESS HORSEMAN

and Other Ghoulish Tales

RETOLD BY MAGGIE PEARSON

ILLUSTRATED BY GAVIN ROWE

Crocodile Books, USA

An imprint of Interlink Publishing Group, Inc.

NEW YORK • NORTHAMPTON

Introduction

Why do we enjoy scary stories? Imagine how it was when these stories were first told. No electricity, just a flickering circle of candlelight, or the campfire. Beyond that, the darkness, full of strange shadows and frightening noises. The storyteller's gift was to draw these unseen monsters into the light, give them a shape and bind them safely into a tale with a beginning, a middle, and a satisfying end.

Some of these stories are found all over the world: the monster in the graveyard or the lake, the headless ghost, the handsome bridegroom who is not all that he seems. The tale, "Abena and the Python" is not so very different from "Bluebeard," and you may have come across Jeannot's ogre in the adventures of Odysseus, or Sinbad the Sailor. Others, like "Skeleton Woman," or "The Road to Samarra," are very special to the culture where the stories were first told.

Listening, you know that the brave and the good and the clever will always win through. But will they this time? Will Vasilissa escape from Baba Yaga? Will the poor man's youngest son outthink the Devil himself? Only the storyteller knows for sure, until the story is ended.

Try and imagine how it must have been in the early days, sitting around the campfire, with only the storyteller's words protecting you from the darkness. And don't have nightmares!

Maggie Pearson

Contents

The Brave Little Tailor

"Monsters!" said the tailor. "There are no such things!"

"There are so!" said the blacksmith, slamming his mug down on the table so hard, it was lucky it was empty, or there'd have been beer flying everywhere.

The butcher and the baker nodded their heads and looked wise. They didn't know about monsters, but they did know the smith was not a man to argue with.

"I say there are not," said the tailor. "Have you ever seen one?"

All three shook their heads, but, as the baker pointed out, he'd never seen China either, yet he was pretty sure it was there.

"A man could travel to China and back," said the tailor, "and never see the least little thing that would in any way pass for a monster."

"No need to go so far," said the butcher. "They say a man has only to spend the night in our own churchyard. Then he'd see!"

"See what?" demanded the tailor.

Ah! That was the question! No one had ever been brave enough to find out. "Dear, dear," said the tailor. "I'd go myself this very night, only I have to sew a pair of trousers for his Lordship the Macdonald, to be delivered first thing in the morning."

"That's no problem," said the smith. "A tailor can take his work anywhere. I'll bring you your needle and thread."

"And how shall I see what I'm doing?" the tailor asked. "It's terrible dark up there in the churchyard."

"No problem," said the baker. "I'll bring a candle to light you."

"And where shall I sit? Those gravestones are terrible cold and hard!"

"No problem at all," said the butcher. "I'll bring you a nice soft cushion to sit on."

Argue he might and argue he did, but come closing time the tailor found himself being marched by the three of them up the hill to the churchyard. And there with his candle and his cushion, his needle and thread and his Lordship's trousers, all cut out and ready to sew, they left him.

The tailor knew it was no good trying to sneak off home. They were sure to be waiting for him somewhere along the road. There was nothing he could do but sit and sew.

He hadn't been sewing for long before the whole churchyard began to shake.

The tailor kept on sewing.

On the wall in front of him, the candle cast the shadow of an enormous head, rising out of the ground. And a deep voice behind him thundered: "Do you see this head?"

The tailor didn't raise his head from his work. "I'll see that," he said, "when I've sewn this."

The head kept rising out of the ground until the tailor could see the shadow of a thick neck under it.

But he kept on sewing.

The voice shouted, "Do you see this neck?"

"I'll see that," said the tailor, "when I've sewn this."

The head and neck went on rising higher and higher, until a great arm heaved itself out of the ground. The tailor could see its shadow on the wall. But he kept on sewing, faster than ever.

"Do you see this arm?" roared the voice.

"I'll see that," said the tailor, "when I've sewn this."

The shadow of the monster was still rising up. It lifted its other arm out of the ground, and began heaving up its body.

The tailor was sewing now for dear life, the needle flying back and forth.

"Do you see this body?"

"I'll see that when I've sewn this."

And the body kept rising up, higher and higher, until it lifted one leg out of the ground.

The tailor was sewing so fast, you couldn't see the needle in the candlelight.

"Do you see this leg?" growled the voice again.

"I'll see that when I've sewn this."

Now the creature was lifting its second leg out of the ground, and it was going to get him for certain, but the tailor came to the end of his sewing, broke off the thread, blew out the candle, jumped over the churchyard wall, and ran off, lickety-split, down the road to his Lordship's castle, with the monster pounding at his heels.

"Open the gate!" yelled the tailor, as he came in sight of the castle walls. "Open the gate and let me in!"

The watchmen, very surprised to see the tailor coming so early in the morning to deliver his Lordship's new trousers – and in such a hurry, too – opened up the gate.

The tailor ran in and the gate closed behind him, not a moment too soon.

The monster was brought up so short he slammed his hand against the wall to save himself from bumping his nose. The marks of his fingers are there to this day.

His Lordship the Macdonald thanked the tailor for his trousers and for delivering them so promptly.

If he noticed a few of the stitches were a bit on the long side, just before the thread was fastened off, he said not a word more about it than the tailor said afterwards when the talk turned to monsters. On that subject, you might say the tailor was as quiet as the graveyard – but he was a lot quieter than that!

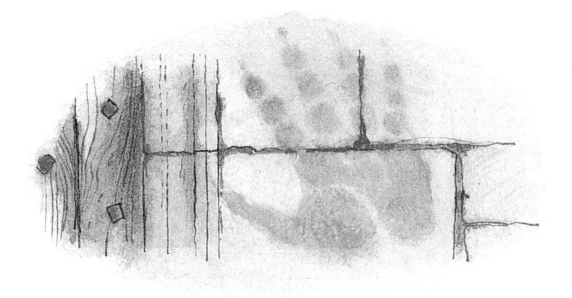

The Bunyip

He used to be a man once, in the old time – the Dreamtime. Then he did something really bad and he clean forgot how to hold on to his man's shape, just thinking all the time about that bad thing he had done. So now he's the bunyip, who's any shape and no shape at all. See that shadow there? Could be the bunyip coming to get you! See that thing moving under the water, way too big to be a fish? That's him all right. Better run. Better hide. What will he do if he catches you? Who knows? No one he caught ever lived to tell the tale.

In the old time – not so long ago as the Dreamtime, maybe, but still a long way back – a bunch of men went hunting. Day in, day out, they hunted and got nothing. They were feeling hungry and they wanted to go home. They couldn't go back with nothing. Their lives wouldn't be worth living. So they sat themselves down by a billabong and cooled their feet in the water, while they wondered what to do next.

Perhaps if they could catch a few fish? Their women wouldn't be so mad at them then for going off hunting for all that time and coming back with nothing to eat. So they started to fish in the deep, dark waters of the billabong.

They caught nothing. It was as bad as the hunting.

"Seems to me," one of them said, "there's something in here that's already eaten all the fish."

While they were still wondering what that something could be, the youngest one yelled out, "I've got a bite!"

He pulled in his line and they all gathered round to see what he'd caught. What was it? It wasn't a fish, that was for sure. It wasn't a baby crocodile, nor an eel, nor any sort of animal they could think of.

"You know what I reckon?" one of them, the oldest, said at last. "I reckon you've caught yourself a bunyip."

"A bunyip? This little thing?" the young man laughed.

"We all start off small," the old man said wisely. "Now throw it back."

"Tide's coming in," said another man. "We'd better be going."

Nobody stopped to wonder why the tide would be coming in, so far from the sea – no river, nothing to fill up that billabong, except when it rained. The water was rising fast. So the men gathered up their stuff and off they went.

Last of all came the youth, carrying the baby bunyip. He couldn't bring himself to toss it back into the water. He didn't think all bunyips could be as bad as people said. If you caught one like this, when it was little, then why shouldn't you keep it, just the same as a dog?

On they went, towards home.

And after them came the water.

They looked back once, and saw that it was flooding the path just behind them, looked again, and it was busy drowning the bushes where they'd been just a minute before.

They started to run, but the water was still coming – and not just the water! There was a big, dark, shapeless thing rising up out of it, and roaring as it came.

The bunyip! But this one was full grown, and it was angry!

The men were running for their lives now. After them, coming just as fast, was the water, swirling and bubbling, covering the rocks and the trees.

And in the middle of it the bunyip raged.

The little bunyip squirmed and wriggled against the youth's chest.

"You want to grow up to be like him?" the young man whispered to it as he ran. "You stick with me. I'll turn you into something better."

Back at the camp the people all came tumbling out of their humpies to see what the fuss was about. They saw the men running and the water tumbling after them, but they couldn't take their eyes off the bunyip. The noise of its roaring filled their heads. They turned to run, but there was nowhere to go. It seemed as if the whole world would soon be covered with water. Already it was up to their ankles, then their knees – and soon it would be up to their chests.

Then the old man saw what the young one was holding up so carefully out of the water. The baby bunyip!

"I told you to throw it back," he shouted. "Do it now!"

The young man did as he was told. He dropped the baby bunyip into the water, and watched it dog paddle away through the flood until it was close enough for the big one to scoop up.

And that old bunyip stopped roaring and started to coo – yes he did!

Then, with the little bunyip safe in his arms again, he just turned away, back towards the billabong, taking the waters with him.

So maybe the bunyip isn't so bad after all. He only did what any dad would have done, if someone tried to take his son away from him.

But that bunyip gave the people such a fright that they were never the same again. Long after their feet should have touched the bottom, they went on paddling. They bent their necks and looked at themselves in what remained of the water, and they saw the reason why. They weren't people any more. They were swans. Black swans.

And swans they stayed. But if you creep down to the billabong after dark and listen to the sound the black swans make, you'd swear for certain that it's people talking.

Skeleton Woman

Far to the north, where there is only ice and snow and gray-blue sky over a gray-blue sea, a little boat bobbed on the water. In the boat sat a fisherman. He had caught nothing all day, but still he sat, fishing. One fish would do, just for himself. He had no one else to feed – there was no one to worry if he came home late, nor anyone to care if he didn't come home at all. A small tear crept from the corner of his eye and rolled down his cheek when he thought of that. He brushed it quickly away and went on fishing.

Suddenly, he felt a tug at his line! He'd caught something. It was a fair size, too, he could see, as he carefully drew it in. Bigger than most fish, but smaller than a seal. And white – purest white. What was it, moving under the water? It looked almost like a woman.

A skeleton woman!

Up she popped out of the water, not an inch from his nose, grinning at him over the side of the tiny boat, her bony fingers scrabbling to catch hold. How long had she lain on the sea bed, rocked by the ocean currents, the big fish nibbling the flesh from her bones, and the little ones playing in and out between her ribs? She didn't know. She only knew how good it felt to be back once more in the world of the living!

"Go away!" cried the fisherman in fear. He dropped his fishing line and grabbed his paddle and hit her again and again until she let go of the boat. Then he paddled as fast as he could for the shore.

After him came Skeleton Woman, waving her bony arms as if to say, "Wait for me, wait for me!"

The man paddled faster, and Skeleton Woman came running after him across the water, legs rattling, head tossing from side to side.

"Wait for me!"

When he reached the shore, the fisherman jumped out of his boat, caught up his fishing tackle, and ran and ran over the snow and the icy waste until he reached home.

He crawled inside, his heart beating like a drum, safe at last, hidden away in his white snow house amid the white, white snow.

After a little while he felt better. He set about untangling his fishing line, and winding it into a neat ball.

Then he heard the rattling of bones outside, and Skeleton Woman came creeping into the snow house after him!

The fisherman stopped working, his heart pounding like a drum again. And Skeleton Woman was still, too. She sat, waiting patiently, a bundle of bones, and he saw what had happened. She couldn't see him, for the fish had long ago eaten her eyes. She couldn't even hear him, for she had no ears. He'd brought her with him, all tangled up in his fishing line.

The fisherman felt sorry for her. So very quietly, very gently, he began to untangle her. It took a long time.

But at last he had her bones laid out, the way a woman's bones should be. Then he crawled back to his own side of the little snow house.

Skeleton Woman rose from the ground where the fisherman had lain her and sat there, her bones rattling together from cold and fear, until he threw her a bundle of furs. "Wrap yourself in those," he said, "and let me get some sleep!"

While the fisherman slept, another tear of loneliness trickled slowly from the corner of his eye.

Skeleton Woman couldn't see or smell or hear – but she could sense his weeping. And she was so thirsty. She crept closer to the man, and she began to drink. And that single tear became a river, full of the water of life. She lay on his chest, and she could hear his heart beating, beating like a drum. And the beat of the drum vibrated through her bones, like a song, singing flesh on her bones and hair on her head and eyes to see and ears to hear – and a heart of her own that went on beating, beating . . .

When the man awoke, there was no
Skeleton Woman – but a real, living one,
and he knew he would never be lonely
again.

   They lived together until the day they
died, and the creatures that had fed on
skeleton woman while she lay under the sea
made sure that the two of them never went
hungry again.

   The people of the northland tell this tale –
and they swear it is true!

The Shadow

A scholar came from the cold northlands to live in the sunny south. Naturally, his shadow came too. The change did them both good. By day they sheltered in the shade, where the air was cool. Then, as the sun went down and the lamps were lit, they would stretch themselves and wander out, side by side at first. But then the shadow began to run ahead, or lag behind, to take a better look at something his master had missed – even climbing up walls to have a peep at what was on the other side.

One evening, the scholar said: "Go on, then, go and enjoy yourself on your own!"

The shadow didn't need telling twice. The scholar felt a little tug at his heels, then the shadow was off and away.

By the next evening it hadn't come back, nor the next, nor any evening after that. Sadly the scholar traveled back to the gray northlands where a man with no shadow wouldn't be noticed much.

Years passed. Late one evening there came a knock at the scholar's door. Outside stood a tall, handsome, dark man, dressed all in black.

"Remember me?" the man said. "I used to be your shadow."

"Oh!" The scholar was quite overcome. "I'm so pleased to see you. I knew you'd come back in the end."

With a lordly smile, the shadow shook his head. "No, no! I don't want my old job back. I'm thinking of traveling south again. I thought you might like to come too."

"I would, indeed," said the scholar.

So the two of them set off, traveling side by side, but this time the warm sun seemed to do the man no good at all. With each day, as evening came, the shadow grew taller, stronger, and more lively, while the man huddled in a corner, almost unnoticed.

Every night the shadow talked, wining and dining with all the best people. He danced with fine ladies, and even with a princess. The princess had always thought she was light on her feet, but this man was lighter still. His feet hardly seemed to touch the ground. He was so graceful – so handsome, and so mysterious, dressed as he always was in solemn black. But where was his shadow?

"My shadow?" The shadow smiled. "See that little fellow in the corner? That's my shadow. I let him dress up like a man, but anyone can see he's just a shadow. Don't tell him, though. You'll hurt his feelings."

"How kind he is!" the princess thought. "But is he wise?" She was more than half in love with the shadow already, but the man she married must be wise, for he would be king one day.

She began asking him all sorts of questions. "Why is the sea salty? Why is the sky blue?" That sort of thing. The shadow didn't know and didn't care, but he was clever enough not to say so.

"I studied all those things long, long ago," he shrugged. "Even my shadow could tell you the answers, if you ask him."

The poor scholar was so pleased to have someone taking notice of him for a change. He answered all the princess's questions.

"How wise my love is!" she thought to herself as she came away. "Even his shadow is wise. This is the man for me!"

When the scholar heard that the princess and his own shadow were going to be married, he knew things had gone far enough.

"This must stop," he told the shadow. "If you don't tell her the truth, then I will!"

The shadow shook his head. "She won't believe you."

She didn't. When the scholar told her that he was the man and the other his shadow, she said he must be mad, and sent for the guards to throw him into the deepest, darkest dungeon.

"It's my fault," said the shadow sadly, when she told him. "I should never have let him pretend to be a man. I must live without a shadow from now on. Can you still love me, without my shadow?"

Of course she could!

Soon afterwards they were married. The bells rang. The bands played. There were fireworks and there was dancing. But the poor scholar heard none of it. He had already become, as the saying goes, no more than a shadow of his former self, lost now among the other shadows in the deepest, darkest dungeon.

He simply faded away, until there was nothing left but a sigh.

The Buried Moon

Night after night Moon shone down on the world and found it beautiful. Winter and summer, over land and sea, she shed her gentle light, over fields and hedgerows, and over cottages with smoke idling from their chimneys. Animals moved quietly in the fields in her light and men ambled home, unafraid.

But when the clouds covered her face and she could see nothing beneath her, Moon often wondered what was happening on Earth. So one night she wrapped herself in a cloak of darkest night and drew up the hood to cover her star-bright hair. A single moonbeam shone from her silvery feet. Down this she walked, from Heaven to Earth.

Moon looked around her. Where were the hedgerows and the pretty little winding streams? Where were the cottages and the animals standing by? Not here. This was an evil place she had come to. The marshlands. Like a bad housewife, Earth sweeps all her rubbish into dark corners and under stones – bogles and boggarts, hobgoblins and hobyars, pookhahs and will o'the'wisps and shapeless things that no man can put a name to.

First Moon smelled them, the cold damp smell of decay. Then she heard them, the whisperings and moanings and shrieks in the night.

Then, creeping and crawling out of the marsh, the slithery, slimy things came to seek her out. And before she could hurry away from that place, something caught her by the foot and would not let go. She cried out – and heard an answering cry!

A traveler, lost in the marshes, came splashing towards her, through slime-covered pools and across narrow paths that shifted and sank beneath his feet. Not this way! This way only led deeper into the marsh. Moon threw back her hood so the traveler could see his way, and all the creeping horrors slid back into their holes.

She could have cried out to the traveler to release her trapped foot, but she never thought of it until he was gone. So she went on trying to free herself from the roots that held her until the hood fell back over her face again. In the darkness, the slithery, slimy things took courage and once more came creeping out of their holes, angry with Moon for spoiling the fun they had meant to have with the traveler before dragging him down to his death.

They pinched her and they punched her. They laid a great stone over her so she could not escape, and set a dead tree there to stand sentinel. They teased her and tormented her until morning came and the first beams of Sun chased them back into their hidy holes.

There Moon lay, night after night, while men looked up at the sky and wondered. The sky was clear, the stars were out. Where was Moon? A group of them went to the wise woman who lived on the edge of the marsh, and they asked her, "Where has Moon gone? What can we do to bring her back?"

"Don't ask me," said the wise woman. "It's a thing that's never happened before, so how can I tell you the way to set it right again?"

The men went away, wondering what to do next. They went on wondering, until one day they heard of a traveler who had been lost so deep on the marsh that he expected to find nothing but his grave. He had been saved by a bright light shining across the water. They told the wise woman this, and she said, "Why, it's as clear as day. Moon is trapped somewhere out there on the marsh. But you'll never find her by daylight."

What! Go by night to where the creeping things were lying in wait, to snatch and cling and spread out carpets of smooth moss that would turn into a bog and suck them down the moment they set foot upon it?

"You'll be safe enough if you do three things," said the wise woman. "Firstly, you must each carry a branch of hazel in your hand. Secondly, you must each have a pebble in your mouth and speak not one word till you have found her. Thirdly, you must look neither left nor right, nor behind you, but walk straight on, until you come to a cross, a coffin, and a candle."

"What then?"

"Then you will know what to do."

As soon as night fell, off they went, each man with a branch of hazel in his hand and a pebble in his mouth. The hardest part was never to look behind, nor left, nor right, knowing all the time that the slithery, slimy creatures of the night were out there, watching and waiting . . .

On went the men, to the very heart of the marsh, until they came to a dead tree, spreading its branches wide in the shape of a cross. At the foot of it a faint radiance shone, like candlelight, from under a heavy stone in the shape of a coffin.

This was the place!

Together they pushed and heaved at the stone, and lifted it a little until the candlelight glowed brighter and became as strong as lamplight. Harder they pushed and heaved, until the glow was like sunlight in deep woods. Even harder still they pushed until the stone tipped right over and they were almost blinded by the brightness of Moon as she leaped up into the sky.

Moon was still a little afraid. She did not show her whole face in the sky, but peeped around the corner of her hooded cloak. Tomorrow she would feel a little braver.

The next day, braver still.

The men bowed to the new Moon. Those who had money in their pockets took it out, turned it over, and put it back again. Then they all turned around three times (for it was safe to turn around now the creatures of the night had all crawled back to their holes), and each of them made a wish. Not one of them spoke his wish aloud, but it's almost certain that they all wished for the same thing.

And that thing came true, for from that day to this, Moon has stayed safely up in the sky, and never gone on her travels again.

Abena and the Python

Abena, she was beautiful. Abena, she could sing so sweet she'd charm the birds right off the trees. Abena, she was proud as any queen.

Young men came courting her every day, almost, but proud Abena just laughed at them. This one was so tall she could use him for a beanpole. That one's ears were so big she'd have to peg him down every time the wind blew, so he didn't fly away.

The young men all went home again, feeling sad.

Abena decided she wasn't going to marry anyone but a prince.

Her parents shook their heads and sighed, "Abena, we're just ordinary folk." But Abena sat waiting for her prince to come and carry her off to his kingdom, far, far away. She made up songs about him. Graceful he'd be, as the long grass swaying in the wind, his voice sweet as the taste of honeydew and his eyes green and bright as emeralds. The little birds listened to her song and they carried it with them as they flew east, west, north, and south.

One day a young man came, treading smoothly and silently across the plain, and shimmering in the midday sun, so that Abena wondered at first whether this was not just a mirage. Gracefully, as the long grass swaying in the wind, he moved, his voice like the taste of honeydew in her mouth, and his eyes green and bright as emeralds.

And he was a prince – so he said –
of a place far, far away.

If Abena hadn't been so picky
before, her parents might have wanted to know a
bit more about him. Why would a prince come all this
way, and all alone, too, just to make Abena his wife?
But married they were, and Abena and her fine new
husband set off towards his kingdom, with food for the
journey, seed corn to plant when they got there, some pigs,
sheep, and a couple of cows.

On the first night, when they stopped to rest, Abena's
new husband ate up all the food. On the second night he

swallowed the seed corn. On the third, fourth, and fifth nights the pigs, sheep and the cows went the same way. Poor Abena got nothing but a few berries she had managed to pick as they went along.

Her new husband grew no fatter with all that food inside him, but it did seem to weigh him down. Closer and closer to the ground he crept, but he was still as graceful as the long grass waving in the winds as he wove his way between rocks and stones, while poor Abena stumbled over them, her tired feet scratched and bleeding.

They came to the forest, and still her husband wove his way, under and over and in between twisting branches and trailing vines, scarcely stirring the leaves, leaving Abena to follow as best she could.

At last they came to a dank, dark river, the waters snaking slow and silent, with no place to cross that Abena could see.

"Where to, now?" she asked.

"Nowhere," he hissed. "This is my kingdom."

In the single patch of sunlight that crept through the leaves overhead, he stretched himself out on a branch above the dead, dark water, twirling his tail around it.

His tail? For Abena's new husband wasn't a man at all but an enormous python! Only his eyes were the same as before, shining cold and hard as emeralds.

"Welcome to your new home," he said, flicking his tongue towards a hole in the riverbank. Abena peeped inside. She saw spiders crouching, watching her from their webs, and beetles scuttling to and fro, and worms creeping across the floor and under it.

"I can't live in there!" she gasped.

"You can!" hissed the python. "You will, for you are my wife!"

Two big tears rolled down Abena's cheeks.

"You told me you were a prince," she sobbed.

"I am," he whispered. "This is my kingdom. Everyone here obeys me – and so will you."

Poor Abena. What would happen to her in this dark, lonely place if she didn't do as he said? Would he wrap his great python body around her and squeeze the life out of her, one breath at a time? Would he just swallow her alive? Abena didn't want to find out. She crawled into that horrible, dark, damp, muddy hole in the riverbank.

And there she stayed.

Every day, when the sun shone through the leaves, the python twined himself round his favorite branch and called the forest animals to come and admire his beautiful human wife. "She's almost as beautiful as me!" he boasted.

The animals were sorry for Abena, but what could they do? The python could swallow them whole, as soon as look at them.

Sometimes they brought her little presents of food. Sometimes the river washed up a fish for her to eat, but there was no fire to cook it on. The rest of the time she nibbled the roots that hung down through the ceiling. When they were gone she often got so hungry that she even ate the slugs and beetles that crawled across the floor.

It was a different song Abena sang nowadays – so sad, so sorry! Singing of her home, so far away, and all the young men she might have married if only she hadn't been so proud.

The birds fluttered down to listen, and they carried her song east, west, north, and south, until one day one of them came to the place where Abena's mother and father lived.

Abena's parents heard the bird's song and they understood. Abena needed their help. They fetched their neighbors and, carrying axes and knives and clubs, followed the bird until at last they came to the banks of that deep, dark river.

They heard their daughter singing her sad songs from her dank hole in the riverbank. They saw the python, twined around his branch, and recognized him by the glow of his emerald eyes.

They made short work of him – yes they did! They beat him till he was stone dead. Then they hacked his branch clean off the tree and watched the river carry it away with the python's bleeding body still twined around it.

From out of her prison they took Abena. She was so thin and bent she seemed like an old, old woman. They carried her home and fed her up until she was as beautiful as the day she went away. But she was not the same, proud Abena anymore. If any young man – or an old one, come to that – had asked her to be his wife, she'd have married him, yes she would!

But no one ever did. For who would want to marry the girl who had been a python's bride?

Bluebeard

He was handsome, rich, and clever, and his beard was of the brightest blue. And he wanted to marry Lady Mary!

Marry a man with a blue beard? Never! Whenever Bluebeard came calling, Lady Mary hid herself away with her sister, Anne, hoping their giggles wouldn't give them away.

Bluebeard was patient. He invited the whole family to visit him. And when Lady Mary saw the fine castle where he lived and the land that he owned, stretching away on every side to the far horizon, she decided that a blue beard was something she could probably get used to.

So they were married. Soon afterwards, Bluebeard had to travel away on the King's business. He gave Lady Mary his keys, saying, "My home is your home. Go into any room you wish, except for the one at the end of the great hall." Then off he went.

Sister Anne came to keep Lady Mary company, and together they roamed all over the castle, upstairs and down, from the attic to the cellar, admiring the furniture, the pictures, the tapestries, and the view from every window. But every time Lady Mary passed the door of the room at the end of the great hall, it seemed to be whispering to her, "Open me! Open me! Bluebeard will never know."

It was easy to see which key fitted the lock. It was the smallest one of all. Surely her husband would never know if she took just one quick peep inside?

So she did. At first she could see nothing. Then, as her eyes became used to the dark, she saw a pile of ladies' shoes. And then a heap of dresses. And the dresses and shoes were all stained with blood. Worst of all, there was a little heap of wedding rings – one, two, three, four – more than she could count.

Her eyes widened in horror. How many times had Bluebeard married before? How many wives had he killed?

Lady Mary slammed the door, and made haste to lock it. Then she noticed that the little key was stained with blood. As fast as she rubbed the blood away with her handkerchief, it came back again. Helter-skelter she ran, down the corridor to the kitchen. There she washed the key and scrubbed it. She scoured it with horsehair and rubbed it with ashes. She wrapped it in cobwebs to stop the flow, but the key went on weeping tears of blood.

"Oh, Mary, I hear Bluebeard returning," cried her sister, and sure enough, there was Bluebeard's voice, calling for her.

In a panic, Lady Mary ran upstairs to change her blood-stained dress and hide the little key on the top shelf of her wardrobe. It was so very, very small.

Perhaps he wouldn't notice for a while that it was missing? But he did. Bluebeard took one look at the great bunch of keys when she handed them back to him, felt the weight of it, and said, "You have been where you had no right to be. You have seen things you were not supposed to see."

Poor Lady Mary, pale as death and trembling like a leaf from head to toe, tried to tell him it wasn't so. The key was so small that she must have dropped it somewhere.

"Then we must find it," said Bluebeard. "Without delay."

He flung open the door of the wardrobe, and there were all her fine dresses, drenched in blood from the little key, drip-dripping from the shelf above.

"Good," said Bluebeard. "Now we have found it, you can join the rest of my wives."

He seized her by the hair and drew his sword.

"Please," she begged him. "Give me a little while to say my prayers before I die! An hour, no more."

In an hour, she knew, her brothers would be there, to fetch home her sister, Anne.

"An hour?" he roared. "No!"

"Half an hour, then. A quarter."

"I'll give you one half of one quarter of an hour."

As soon as she was left alone, Lady Mary called out softly to her sister, who was watching from the tower for their brothers to arrive.

"Sister Anne, what can you see?"

Sister Anne answered, "Only the sun and the green grass and the dusty road."

The minutes ticked by, but every time Lady Mary called out, the answer was always the same.

"Only the sun and the green grass and the dusty road."

Now she could hear her husband, climbing the stairs.

"Sister Anne, what can you see?"

"Only the sun and the green grass – and a great cloud of dust in the distance."

"Is it our brothers?"

"No, just a flock of sheep."

Now Lady Mary could hear Bluebeard's footsteps coming along the passage.

"Sister Anne, what can you see?"

"I see the sun and the green grass – and a small cloud of dust in the distance. It is two horsemen."

But now Lady Mary could hear Bluebeard outside the door, sharpening his sword on the stone portal.

"Is it our brothers?"

"Yes it is – and galloping fast!"

Bluebeard was turning the key in the lock, flinging open the door. In two strides he was there beside her.

Lady Mary gave such a shriek that her two brothers heard her as they reached the castle gate.

Bluebeard grasped her by the hair, and lifted up his sword.

The brothers galloped straight in and up the stairs. Between the time Bluebeard took to raise his sword and bring it down again to strike Lady Mary's head from her shoulders, they were in the room to save her.

When they had finished with Bluebeard, what was left of him was hardly fit to be thrown to the dogs. The little birds pecked the flesh from his bones and plucked the blue hairs of his beard to line their nests.

And Lady Mary left that terrible place, never to return.

The Headless Horseman

At the dead hour of night, when the shadows are deepest and the stars burn brightest and the wind whips the clouds across the face of the moon, the headless horseman rides down through Sleepy Hollow.

Horsefeathers! I hear you say. But try riding that road alone, by night, when every whip-o-will's cry sounds like a poor, lost soul, and the glowworms are like so many eyes winking, and the rustling of the branches like dead men's bones, you'll be listening for the sound of hoofbeats on the road behind you.

That's how it was with Ichabod Crane, who used to be the schoolmaster in those parts. An educated man, a sensible man – except when he happened to be riding home by night through Sleepy Hollow. At those times he used to sing to himself, to keep his courage up. A fine voice he had: there were times when the rest of the choir in the church on a Sunday were left open-mouthed, leaving him to sing on by himself.

And he could dance! Whenever he stepped onto the floor, the servants would cluster in windows and doorways, just for a sight of Ichabod Crane a-leaping and a-capering.

Ichabod wasn't planning to be a schoolmaster all his life. He'd set his sights on Katerina van Tassel, whose father was the richest farmer in the area.

Katerina didn't say yes and she didn't say no. But she smiled at Ichabod so prettily that Brom Bones – who'd decided she was the girl for him since the day he gave her his pet frog for a birthday present, and she tipped him in the horse trough for stuffing it down her neck – Brom Bones felt black jealousy stirring in his heart every time he saw her smile at Ichabod Crane.

At the Hallowe'en dance in van Tassel's barn, Ichabod leapt and spun fit to leave a whirlwind standing. His singing woke all the little birds roosting in the rafters. When the fireside talk turned to ghost stories, Ichabod had a few of those to tell, too.

Then Brom Bones got up and said: "Did you ever hear of the headless horseman of Sleepy Hollow?"

Ichabod said that he had.

"Did you ever meet him?" demanded Brom Bones. "I did, last fall, as I was riding home. He didn't scare me none! I offered to race him. I'd have beaten him, too. But when we reached the bridge over the stream, he vanished in a flash of fire!"

"Really?" said Ichabod.

"Really!" declared Brom Bones. "As sure as I'm standing here to tell the tale!"

"How brave!" sighed Katerina, turning to Brom with shining eyes.

"Huh!" said Ichabod, who didn't believe a word of it – at least, not until he took his lonely road home later that night through Sleepy Hollow. The night seemed darker than usual. He heard the owl scream and the crickets cry. He tried to sing a little song to keep his spirits up, but his voice went all wobbly and frightened him still more.

It should have been a relief to see another rider, falling into step beside him, taking the same road home, but somehow it wasn't. There was something not quite right about this one.

"Good evening to you!" said Ichabod, wishing his voice wasn't quite so wobbly.

No answer.

"Were you at van Tassel's party tonight?"

Still no answer.

"It's a fine night to be riding home. Very mild for the time of year!"

Still nothing.

Then Ichabod nudged his horse with his heels, urging it to go faster.

The other rider was still right beside him, and he reined in, so the other could ride ahead. But he didn't.

Side by side they rode on, not speaking. Then the moon rolled out from behind a cloud, and Ichabod could see his companion more clearly. He was a tall man, with broad shoulders on him.

And no head!

Ichabod gave a wild cry, clapped spurs to his horse, and was off at a gallop. But the other was there, with a wild "Halloo!" right on his tail.

On they galloped through Sleepy Hollow, Ichabod Crane and the headless horseman right behind, both going like the wind down towards the rickety bridge.

What was it Brom Bones had told him about the bridge on the night Brom had challenged the headless horseman to a race? The moment they reached the bridge, the ghost had vanished in a flash of fire!

All Ichabod had to do was to reach the bridge. After him galloped the horseman, hot breath on his neck now, and the thunder of ghostly hooves in his ears. As Ichabod reached the bridge he risked a look behind him, and saw the horseman take his severed head from under his cloak and fling it through the air towards him!

Next day Ichabod's horse was found, quietly cropping the grass near the bridge. And all that was left of Ichabod Crane was his hat, which lay close by. They also found a Halloween pumpkin with eyes and mouth carved in it – though what that had to do with the schoolmaster's strange disappearance was anyone's guess.

Not long afterwards, Katerina married Brom Bones, as she'd always meant to do.

Some people say that Ichabod Crane just left town that night when he realized Katerina wouldn't have him, but others think they know better. They say the headless horseman got him. They say that if you dare to ride down through Sleepy Hollow at the dark, dead hour of night and listen for the sound of hoofbeats, you may also hear the voice of Ichabod Crane, singing a little song to keep his spirits up.

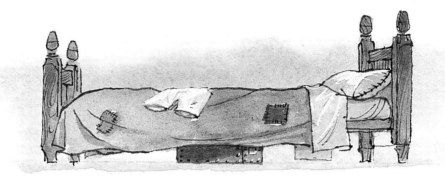

A Bargain is a Bargain

There was a poor man whose wife had died, leaving him with three young sons. He did his best to be both father and mother to them. By day he took whatever work was going, so he could earn enough to keep them all. In the evenings he cooked and cleaned, mended their clothes for them, and told them stories. But it was hard work.

He had just one wish in all the world, and that was that his sons would have easier lives than his. Whenever he could, he tucked a bit of money away in the old chest he kept under the bed. One day he hoped he'd have enough to send them off to school. The trouble was that money never stayed saved long enough to amount to anything. There was always one of the boys needing new shoes, or they'd run out of potatoes or turnips and needed another sackful. Growing boys couldn't live on air.

"Oh, I would give myself body and soul if I could just save enough to put my three boys through school," cried the man one day, as he closed the lid of the chest again, leaving it lighter by the price of a jug of milk.

"Would you so?" came a soft voice from the corner of the room. "Body and soul, you said?"

The man turned and saw that, though the door and windows were locked, there was a man standing there, dressed all in black, save for the scarlet lining to his cloak. He's a snappy dresser, Old Nick.

"Would you really give yourself, body and soul?" repeated Old Nick.

"I would!" the man said, though he knew he was talking to the Devil himself. "I would give myself body and soul if my boys could only go to school!"

"It's a bargain, then," said Old Nick. He held out his hand, so they could shake on it. That hand the man took was as cold as death.

"I'll be back in ten years to collect," said Old Nick.

Then he vanished. When the man looked inside the chest again, there was enough money and more besides, to put all three boys through school.

So off they went. In time, one became a doctor, one a priest, and the third a lawyer.

The man never told the boys about the bargain he'd made, and the boys never thought to ask how their father had saved so much money.

Ten years went by, faster than the poor man would have liked, but that's life. His son the doctor was visiting him one stormy night. The wind was howling round the house and blowing the smoke

back down the chimney.

"Was that a knock at the door I heard?" the doctor asked.

When his father went to open it, there stood Old Nick, with not a drop of rain on his scarlet-lined cloak, billowing behind him.

"What's this?" said the doctor.

"Time to go," said Old Nick.

So then the story had to come out.

"Rubbish!" said the doctor. "My old father's not going to die yet. I've just given him a checkup, and he's as healthy as I am!"

Old Nick was not a bit put out. "Who said anything about dying? If he's to be my slave till the end of time, I want your father fit and well. Body and soul was the bargain."

"Give him a few more days," the doctor begged. "Let him see my brother the priest before he goes."

Maybe the Devil's not all bad.

"A priest will make no difference," he said. "But I'll let you see him so you can say goodbye."

So the doctor sent for his brother the priest, explaining to him how things were.

"Leave this to me," said the priest.

And they sat there waiting, the old man and his son, with the mist creeping round the house, trying to find a way in and sliding at last through the keyhole until there was enough of it to form itself into a man.

"Are you coming now?" asked Old Nick.

"Not so fast!" said the priest. "My father's a good man. He spent not one penny of that money you gave him on himself."

"What's that to me?" said Old Nick. "A bargain's a bargain."

"Here's some of the money that was left," said the priest. "Take it back now and we'll repay the rest."

"I don't want the money," said Old Nick. "Body and soul was the bargain."

"Will you just wait a little longer for my other brother to come home and say goodbye to my father?"

"I can wait," said Old Nick. "What's another week or so, compared with all eternity?"

At last the youngest son – the lawyer – arrived. Outside, the air was cold, so cold your breath would freeze the moment it left your mouth. But the touch of that hand, ten years ago, had been colder still. The lawyer son had hardly set foot inside the door, taken off his coat, and sat down to warm himself beside the fire, when Old Nick was there in the room with him.

"Give us a moment or two, please!" said the lawyer. "I haven't had time to say hello, let alone goodbye."

Old Nick looked doubtful. He knew a tidy few lawyers already, and they were too clever by half.

"See that candle on the table?" said the lawyer. "Just give us until it's burned away."

The Devil looked at the candle and saw there was no more than ten minutes' light left in it.

"All right," he nodded.

"Is that a bargain?"

"It is," said old Nick, sitting himself down. "I'll wait."

"I wouldn't if I were you," smiled the lawyer. "You could be sitting there a long, long time!" With that, he pinched out the candle flame and handed the stub to his father. "There you are, Dad, you just keep that safe. A bargain's a bargain, right?" he said to Old Nick. "Until that candle burns right down, you won't touch my old father!"

Old Nick had to smile, and then he began to laugh, fit to burst. He knew he'd been beaten, fair and square.

The old man kept that stump of candle in his pocket until the day he died, and his three sons made certain sure that it was buried with him. And so, I suppose, he went to heaven.

The priest was a good man, and the doctor a wise one, but it took a lawyer to get the better of Old Nick. Don't you go thinking you can pull the same trick, though. He's wise to that one now. If you take my advice, you'll have no dealings with Old Nick at all. May the Devil always keep one step behind you, all your days!

The Ogre

At the top of the mountain behind the village there lived an ogre who kept a flock of sheep with golden horns. He had teeth like wild boar's tusks and fingers like eagle's claws and one eye in the middle of his forehead.

The villagers knew he ate people, because no one who had ever gone up the mountain had come down again to tell the tale of what they'd found there.

"If no one's come back, then how do they know?" asked Jeannot. "How do they know the ogre eats people? How do they know what he looks like? How do they know there's an ogre there at all?"

Jeannot's mother couldn't think of how to answer these questions. She just told him not to go climbing up the mountain to find out for himself. So he didn't – well, not at first. He just went as far as the first big rock. Carefully, he peered around it. He saw no ogre, no flock of sheep with golden horns – in fact, nothing strange at all.

The next day he went a bit further – as far as the next clump of trees. Still nothing. So, step by step, day by day, Jeannot slowly climbed the mountain – until one day he climbed so high he knew he would have to run all the way back down again if he wanted to get home before it was dark.

Suddenly, by the light of the evening sun, he saw something sparkling in the grass. Jeannot ran forward to look and found a bright, gold-colored, curved sheep's horn. He picked it up. It was so heavy he knew it must be gold. How long could he and his mother live on that much gold? A year? A lifetime? Jeannot didn't know, but he did know that where there was one horn there could well be another, so he put the horn under his arm and walked on, up the mountain, in search of more riches. Round the very next bend he came upon a flock of sheep, quietly grazing. And every one of them had a pair of golden horns.

While Jeannot still stood there, staring in amazement, he felt himself rising into the air. Something had him by the suspenders–

something with teeth like wild boar's tusks,
for he saw them as he was lifted still higher. Something with one
eye in the middle of its forehead!

"Caught you!" the ogre roared. "You little thief!"

"I'm not a thief!" Jeannot yelled back. "I found the horn, lying in
the grass. Finders keepers!"

"Well, now I've found you!" the ogre replied. "And I'm going to
keep you – but not for long. Only until I eat you!"

Still carrying Jeannot by his suspenders, the ogre began rounding up
his sheep and herding them into their pen for the night. When they
were all inside and the gate locked fast, the ogre put the boy down.

He lit himself a fire, killed one of the sheep, skinned it, cooked it and ate it.

After that he lay down to sleep, while Jeannot sat trembling by the embers of the fire, wondering when he was going to be eaten. Perhaps for breakfast! He had to get away tonight – but how? The gate was bolted fast and the walls were too high to climb.

Jeannot picked up a stick and poked the fire. As he did so, he noticed that the end of it was gradually smoldering away, making a point at one end. He remembered what his mother had said about playing with pointed sticks.

"You could poke someone's eye out with that!"

Jeannot looked at the sleeping ogre with one eye in the middle of his forehead. Then he blew on the fire to make it hotter, and stuck the stick into it until the end was as hard and pointed as a spear. Step by step he crept up to the ogre and thrust the point straight through his eyelid and into the eye. The cry of agony the ogre let out was enough to make Jeannot promise himself that if he ever did get safely home, he'd never play with sharp sticks again.

Jeannot crouched down and hid himself among the sheep, thinking that come morning, the ogre would be letting them out and then he could make his escape.

But, of course, the ogre knew that too. When morning came, he opened the gate just wide enough for one sheep to go through at a time. He felt their woolly coats and he counted them as they went – "One, two, three . . ."

What was Jeannot to do now? Once the sheep were gone, there'd be no one but himself and the ogre, locked in the pen together.

"Twenty-eight, twenty-nine . . ."

Suddenly, Jeannot spotted the skin of the sheep the ogre had killed the night before. He wrapped himself in it – phew, it smelt terrible! – and joined the line of sheep waiting to go through the gate.

"Forty-three, forty-four . . ." the ogre counted. Then he paused. What was this? A sheep? He felt it carefully. It was woolly, like a sheep. He sniffed it. It smelled like a sheep – mostly. But was there just a hint of boy? The ogre's long talons began feeling it all over, down the creature's legs. Then there was just the dead fleece, hanging from the ogre's fingers as Jeannot threw it off. Jeannot dashed through the gate and down the mountainside, running for his life.

After him the ogre pounded, listening for the sound of the stones rattling down the path that would tell him which way the boy had gone.

The rattling stopped.

The ogre stood listening, smelling the air, while Jeannot crouched, still as a mouse.

Slowly, silently, Jeannot reached for a stone and threw it.

The ogre heard it land, and set off after it. Then Jeannot threw another stone – and another. And the monster stumbled after them, arms flailing. Any minute now he'd have that boy! And then he'd tear him limb from limb – but not before he'd roasted him alive!

Which way now? This way? That way? Left, right, or straight on? Another pebble rattled down the cliffside. After it the ogre ran, pell-mell. Straight on he went, at a rush – and right over a cliff! He twisted and turned as he fell, until he reached the bottom with a crash that broke every bone in his body.

When the villagers found the body, they made Jeannot a hero. And when the boy took them all up the mountain the next day and showed them the sheep with the golden horns – enough to make them rich for life – even his mother couldn't be cross with him. But there was a look in her eye that told him he'd better not disobey again. Dealing with a boy-eating ogre is one thing, but dealing with your mother on the warpath is quite another!

The Road To Samarra

A merchant of Baghdad was working in his garden one day when he saw his favorite servant coming towards him. The servant's face was white, his hands were trembling, and his legs seemed scarcely to belong to him.

The merchant hurried to help. He led the poor man to a seat in the shade, fetched him water to drink from the fountain, then sat down beside him.

"What's the matter?" he asked. "Are you ill?"

The servant shook his head.

"What is it then? Tell me when you're ready."

At last the servant was able to speak. "Master," he said, "this morning you sent me down to the market to buy food for supper tonight."

The merchant nodded. "So I did. Was it in the marketplace that something frightened you?"

The man shuddered. "I saw Death standing there. She looked at me and stared so hard! Master, lend me a horse, so that I can ride far, far away, to a place where Death will not find me."

The merchant was fond of his servant, so he didn't argue. He said: "Take the best horse from my stable and ride to where you will. Stay there as long as you want. But where will you go?"

"I have a cousin who lives in Samarra," said the servant. "I'll go there. That's far enough away."

So the merchant led the servant to the stable, and helped him saddle up his finest horse – for the servant's hands were trembling far too much for him to be able to manage it on his own. The merchant gave his servant food and money for the journey, and sent him on his way, galloping down the road to Samarra, where Death would not find him.

Then the merchant went down to the market place and found Death still standing there among the scurrying crowds. The merchant noticed that no one looked at her directly, and they all made a space around her as they hurried by.

The merchant was a wise man, and not afraid to meet Death face to face. He went straight up to her and asked: "Why did you terrify my servant so, when he came here this morning?"

Death smiled. "Did I frighten him?" she asked. "I'm sorry, I didn't mean to stare. But I was just so surprised to see him here in Baghdad, when I am supposed to meet him tonight in Samarra."

The Changeling

A soldier was coming home from the wars, striding along the country lanes and whistling a tune to keep himself in step. Over the seven seas he'd sailed – marched across deserts and over mountains. But nothing he'd seen on all his travels could gladden his heart more than the sight of the house where he'd been born, with his father and mother waiting for him at the door.

Seven years it was since he'd left that place. Six years since they'd written to say his little brother had been born.

Where was the little fellow, then? Where was he?

Still in his cradle? At six years old?

"Doesn't he walk yet?" asked the soldier.

"No, he doesn't walk," his mother sighed.

The soldier leaned over the cradle and looked at the child, and the child looked straight back at him. Little gleaming black eyes in a face as brown and wizened as a walnut.

"Does he talk, then?" the soldier asked.

His father shook his head. "No, he doesn't talk."

"He doesn't thrive, either," said his mother. "He eats a man's portion, but look at him! So thin, poor little dear!"

"He doesn't sleep, you see," said his father. "Night after night he wakes us with his crying."

All the time the soldier was looking at the creature in the cradle, and the creature was looking back at him, and that look was evil, through and through.

"I know what you are," the soldier was thinking. "I know why you don't walk or talk or thrive or sleep. You're a changeling. My little brother's away with the fairies, and they've left you in his place. And it's there you mean to stay, I suppose, like a cuckoo in the nest, worrying my poor parents to a shadow and then into their graves. Well, we'll see about that, we will!"

What could he do? He couldn't say to his mother and father: "That's not my little brother! That's a changeling you've got there!" Not after they'd tended the creature and watched it and worried over it these six years – and he, just back from the wars and setting eyes on it for the first time, thinking he knew better than they did.

Nor could he take it and leave it on the cold hillside for the fairies to fetch away their own before it starved or died of cold. For what would happen to his little brother then?

"I've got you, haven't I?" the creature seemed to say with its wicked, boot-button eyes.

But a plan was forming in the soldier's mind.

"You two go on up to bed," he said to his parents. "Rest easy tonight. I'll watch over the little fellow. I'll smoke a pipe and maybe brew myself a drop of beer."

So his father and mother went to their beds, and the soldier sat smoking his pipe, and all the while the creature was watching him with its beady little eyes.

When the pipe was quite smoked out, the soldier got up and stretched himself.

"Time for that drop of beer," he said.

He took an egg and broke it. Then he threw away the insides and kept the shell.

"Now, what do I do next?" said the soldier to himself. "I know!"

He went out into the garden and came back carrying one hop-flower.

The creature was sitting up in its cradle by now, watching everything he did.

The soldier went to the cupboard and took out three grains of barley. He put these into the eggshell with the hop-flower, and filled the eggshell up with water.

All the while the creature was watching him, hanging over the side of the cradle, to see what he would do next.

The soldier took the fire tongs and, holding the eggshell carefully, he set it on the fire to boil.

Suddenly the creature spoke.

"I'm old, I'm old, three hundred years and more,

But beer brewed in an eggshell I've never seen before!" said the creature.

"Oh, you're old, are you?" said the soldier. "And you can walk, can you? And you can talk, can you? And can you sing?"

He flung the eggshell with the boiling water straight at the evil,

little thing. The creature didn't sing. Nor did it cry like a baby cries. It shrieked like a whistling kettle left too long to boil, like a banshee come to fetch away the dead.

It was heard by the fairies far away in the hills. It was heard by the soldier's father and mother, snug in their beds, and awoken from their first good sleep in a month of Sundays.

Downstairs they came and stood amazed at what they saw.

There was the creature who never stood on its own two legs, nor spoke a word, dancing around the room and calling their soldier son such names as aren't fit to be written down here, and between times, shrieking in its banshee voice. Then it spun itself around till it was spinning like a top, took flight, and vanished up the chimney.

There in its place stood a little boy of six years old, fair-haired, pink-cheeked, and bright-eyed, just as the soldier had always imagined his little brother would be. And he could walk – and talk! Talk about anything, he would, until you were dizzy – anything under the sun, bar one. That was the six years he'd spent away with the fairies. And about that he never spoke a single word.

Vasilissa and Baba Yaga

In a little house on the edge of the forest Vasilissa lived with her father. They were very happy. Then one day he brought home a new wife.

"She'll be company for you when I'm not here," he said.

Vasilissa already had her doll for company. She always gave the girl good advice.

"Never mind," said the doll. "We must make the best of it, that's all."

Vasilissa tried to make the best of things, but her stepmother was horrible. When the father was there, she was all honey and kisses. But as soon as the door closed behind him, it was a very different story. Poor Vasilissa had to clean the house, do the washing, cook the dinner, fetch the firewood and, if any little thing went wrong, it was always her fault – even when the fire went out with the stepmother dozing right beside it.

One day the stepmother said to Vasilissa: "We need a light for the fire. You can fetch it from my sister, who lives in the forest."

Even at midday, the forest was a dark and dismal place.

"No one lives in the forest," whispered Vasilissa. "Except for Baba Yaga, the witch. She has red-hot coals for eyes, and she eats people!"

The stepmother laughed nastily. "What if she does?" she said, and pushed Vasilissa out of the door.

"Don't worry," the doll whispered from Vasilissa's pocket. "I'll look after you."

So Vasilissa set off down the path and into the deep, dark forest. She hadn't been walking for very long when she noticed what looked like an eye winking at her on the path ahead.

"Don't be afraid," said the doll. "An eye can't hurt you."

But when Vasilissa went towards it, she found it wasn't an eye at all, but a little bottle of oil.

"Pick it up," said the doll. "It might come in handy."

So Vasilissa picked up the little bottle and put it in her pocket.

A bit further on, she saw what looked like a trail of blood.

"Blood's just blood," said the doll.

When Vasilissa got closer she saw it wasn't blood after all, but a length of red ribbon.

"Waste not, want not," said the doll.

So Vasilissa tied the red ribbon in her hair and walked on down the path, further and further into the dark forest. It was so dark, she almost tripped over the round, white thing lying in the middle of the path. A skull?

"What if it is?" said the doll. "It won't bite you."

But when Vasilissa looked closer, she found it wasn't a skull at all – just half a loaf of bread.

"Waste not, want not?" asked Vasilissa, picking it up.

"It might come in handy," agreed the doll.

So they went on, and when Vasilissa found some scraps of meat lying in the way, she didn't hesitate. She picked them up and wrapped them in her hankie.

"Good girl," said the doll. "You're learning fast!"

Night was falling when they reached a little house. Though the forest was dark, all around the house it was as bright as day. As Vasilissa drew closer she could see that the fence was made of human bones, and on every post was a human skull, with a light burning inside. When Vasilissa saw that the house stood on two chicken's legs, she knew she had arrived at Baba Yaga's, the witch, who was also the stepmother's sister.

The gate squealed and groaned on its hinges when Vasilissa tried to push it open.

"What a good thing we brought that oil," remarked the doll.

Vasilissa oiled the hinges and the gate swung open of its own accord to let her pass, but a birch tree just inside lashed at her with its branches.

"What now?"

"What now!" said the doll. "We've found a use for that bit of ribbon you picked up."

Vasilissa took the ribbon from her hair and tied the branches back. But she hadn't taken more than a few steps when a skinny-looking dog came bounding out of the house, barking and showing his teeth. Vasilissa threw him the loaf of bread, and he lay down quietly to eat it.

Vasilissa walked up to the door and knocked. It was opened by a cat, as mangy and half-starved as the dog.

"Please," asked Vasilissa. "Is Baba Yaga home?"

"You're in luck," said the cat. "She's out."

"My stepmother sent me for a light," said Vasilissa. "I can't go home without it. Will you help me?"

"Lights are not my business," said the cat. "Mice are my business. I'll starve if I don't catch one soon. Baba Yaga never feeds me."

"I have some meat, wrapped up in my handkerchief," said Vasilissa. "Would you like it?"

"Would I like it," sighed the cat. "Is the sea salt? Is the sky blue? Of course I'd like it!"

So Vasilissa gave the cat the meat, and it said, "Thank you. Take one of the skulls from the fence with the light burning inside, and then run for your life. I can hear Baba Yaga coming."

Sure enough, at the very moment when Vasilissa was snatching the skull from the fence, Baba Yaga was on her way home, rowing herself through the sky in her pestle and mortar – for that is how she always traveled. She noticed the missing skull at once. Who had taken it?

The cat looked up from chewing a piece of meat. "I gave it to Vasilissa," it said. "She gave me meat, when you would let me have none."

"Why didn't you stop her?" Baba Yaga yelled at the dog, at the birch tree, and at the gate.

"Vasilissa gave me some bread," replied the dog. "You gave me nothing but kicks and beatings, in all the years I kept guard for you."

"You never noticed how beautiful I was," sighed the birch tree. "But Vasilissa gave me a red ribbon to wear."

"Life is so easy now," murmured the gate, "since Vasilissa oiled my hinges. Calm down, Baba Yaga. You'll never catch her."

Baba Yaga climbed into her mortar and, rowing madly with her pestle, she went screaming through the sky after Vasilissa. Everyone put up their shutters and barred the doors against the whirlwind. As for Vasilissa, she ran and she ran, until she outpaced Baba Yaga and came safely home.

"Here I am, Stepmother," said Vasilissa. "I've fetched the light, as you asked." She held up the skull and the fire in its eyes burned brighter and brighter still. The stepmother hid her face, but now the light burned so bright and fierce that, with a flash of flame, the stepmother vanished. Nothing was left of her but a little heap of ashes. The door burst open, and the wind carried the ashes away.

After that, Vasilissa and her father lived, just the two of them, in the little house on the edge of the forest. And when her father was away from home, she had her doll for company, just as before.

Cry Wolf

All day and every day, the boy sat on the hillside, watching the sheep. He didn't do it because he liked it. Watching sheep was tedious. But somebody had to watch the sheep and, though he was old enough to work, he wasn't big enough to do much else.

So he sat there, watching them.

"Why?" he asked the shepherd.

"In case the wolf comes and tries to steal one of them for supper."

"What do I do then?"

"You must shout 'Wolf, Wolf!' just as loud as you can, and all the villagers will come running to scare the wolf away."

The boy sat and sat. He was bored, and he almost wished the wolf would come.

What if the wolf did come and he shouted "Wolf! Wolf!" with all his might and nobody heard him, nobody came?

He ought to make sure they could hear. So the boy climbed on a rock, until he could see down into the village and he began to shout, "Wolf! Wolf!"

The villagers heard him. They snatched up sticks and stones and hammers and spades and came running up the hill, pell-mell, to drive that wolf away.

They weren't very pleased when they found there wasn't a wolf.

"I just wanted to make sure you could hear me," said the boy.

So, grumbling loudly, the villagers went away.

The next day the boy became bored again. He remembered what fun it had been to see the villagers all rushing up the hill when he cried "Wolf!" So he did it again.

"Wolf!" he shouted. "Wolf! It's the wolf!"

Up they all ran, stumbling over the rocks, with their sticks and shovels.

"I thought I saw something that might have been a wolf," said the boy. "But it wasn't. I'm sorry."

He wasn't really sorry, though. He was laughing inside to think how easy it had been to make then all run. So the next day

he did it again – and the next – and every day after that, and sometimes twice a day, too.

Meanwhile, not very far off, the wolf sat quietly watching. The first time he heard the boy shout "Wolf!" he started up in alarm, but he didn't run, because no one came near.

The second time, he lay very still in the shadows, but still no one came near. It was the wolf who crept steadily nearer. Each day a little nearer.

He saw how each time it took the villagers a bit longer to run up the mountain path with their sticks and shovels.

And when they went back down the hillside again, he crept just a little bit nearer still.

So the wolf watched and waited until –

"Wolf! Wolf!" cried the boy from high up on the mountain. The villagers down in the valley heard the cry well enough. They looked at one another and they smiled.

"We'll teach that boy a lesson," they said. They shrugged their shoulders and went on with their work.

"Wolf! Wolf!" cried the boy at the top of his voice. The valley re-echoed with the sound. "Wolf, Wo-o-o-oolf!"

Then there was silence.

When the shepherd went to fetch the sheep down for the night he found them all present and correct, grazing peacefully. No sign of a wolf.

Nor any sign of the boy, either!

The End